POCKET STUDY SKILLS

*Series Editor: **Kate Williams**, Oxford Brookes University, UK*
Illustrations by Sallie Godwin

For the time-pushed student, the *Pocket Study Skills* pack a lot of advice into a little book. Each guide focuses on a single crucial aspect of study, giving you step-by-step guidance, handy tips and clear advice on how to approach the important areas which will continually be at the core of your studies.

Published

14 Days to Exam Success
Blogs, Wikis, Podcasts and More
Brilliant Writing Tips for Students
Completing Your PhD
Doing Research
Getting Critical
Planning Your Essay
Planning Your PhD
Reading and Making Notes
Referencing and Understanding Plagiarism
Science Study Skills
Success in Groupwork
Time Management
Writing for University

Further titles in preparation

Pocket Study Skills

Series Standing Order
ISBN 978-0230-21605-1
(outside North America only)

You can receive future titles in this series as they are published by placing a standing order. Please contact your bookseller or, in case of difficulty, write to us at the address below with your name and address, the title of the series and the ISBN quoted above.

Customer Services Department,
Macmillan Distribution Ltd
Houndmills, Basingstoke, Hampshire
RG21 6XS England

TIME MANAGEMENT

POCKET STUDY SKILLS

Kate Williams & Michelle Reid

palgrave
macmillan

First published 2011 by
PALGRAVE MACMILLAN

Palgrave Macmillan in the UK is an imprint of Macmillan Publishers Limited, registered in England, company number 785998, of Houndmills, Basingstoke, Hampshire RG21 6XS.

Palgrave Macmillan in the US is a division of St Martin's Press LLC, 175 Fifth Avenue, New York, NY 10010.

Palgrave Macmillan is the global academic imprint of the above companies and has companies and representatives throughout the world.

Palgrave® and Macmillan® are registered trademarks in the United States, the United Kingdom, Europe and other countries

ISBN-13: 978-0-230-29960-3

This book is printed on paper suitable for recycling and made from fully managed and sustained forest sources. Logging, pulping and manufacturing processes are expected to conform to the environmental regulations of the country of origin.

A catalogue record for this book is available from the British Library.

A catalog record for this book is available from the Library of Congress.

Printed in China

Contents

Acknowledgements

Many people have contributed to this book and we would like to thank them all. The experiences of the students we have worked with form the bedrock of this book, and many of their comments are quoted directly in the margins. These give an insight into both the pressures students work under and the inventiveness of the solutions and strategies students have developed. We pass them on to you …

We have also drawn on the experiences of staff in several countries both in the text and in the comments we capture in the margins. Many thanks to all who contributed their thoughts at various points in the process from inception to critical review:

Marion Casey, Counsellor, Oxford Brookes University, UK

Susan Christopherson, J. Thomas Clark Professor, City and Regional Planning, Cornell University, USA

Gordon Clark (FBA), Halford Mackinder Professor of Geography, University of Oxford, UK for sharing his insights into the time pressures shared by students in the USA, UK and Australia

Betsy Donald, Associate Professor, Department of Geography, Queen's University, Ontario, Canada

Phillip O'Neill, Director, Urban Research Centre, University of Western Sydney, Australia

Jim Pye, Mature Students' Adviser, Oxford Brookes University, UK

Kim Shahabudin, Study Adviser, University of Reading, UK

Michael Webber, Professorial Fellow, Department of Resource Management and Geography, The University of Melbourne, Australia

Our thanks too to Sallie Godwin for her astute illustrations, and to Suzannah Burywood and colleagues in the editing and production teams at Palgrave Macmillan who have been endlessly supportive and creative in making this book happen.

Introduction

Your time at university is a time of change. It is a particular phase of your life that you have chosen and you want to make the most of it. It is a time of opportunity, to learn, to meet people and experience new ideas and ways of doing things and to become in some way a different person at the end of it.

It can also be a pressurised time, where the core business of the university – the modules and courses you take – run to a particular schedule with fixed deadlines and expectations about how you fit into this established pattern. This may come naturally to you, or it may feel stressful, at least to begin with.

I'm terrible at time management – always have been.

I never have enough time to do what I want.

I always leave everything to the last minute – it's just the way I am.

I can't work unless I'm under pressure.

I'm just lazy ... no other explanation.

I know what I need to do – I just can't make myself do it.

But no one is born good or bad at managing their time! The strategies we all employ to do (or avoid doing) something are habits we have developed over the years ... not fixed characteristics.

'Time management' in this book is not about what you *should* be doing and rigid timetables that you will never stick to. It is about finding effective ways of getting things done, putting you in control of your time and making a few small changes to achieve what you want to achieve during your time at university.

About this book

Part 1 Getting it all done suggests some core strategies for getting it all done in the time you have.

Part 2 Getting strategic about time is about taking control, getting informed and finding all the key information you need about your term or semester.

Part 3 Planning the term or semester shows how you can use that information to plan the shape of your term or semester.

Part 4 Troubleshooting Different people have different issues when it comes to time management. Dip in and out for suggestions depending on what you need.

Part 5 What next ...? invites you to review how you used your time in the semester just gone, and to think about any changes you might make in the future.

GETTING IT ALL DONE

Part 1 starts with what's in front of you – how to start organising your current tasks, files and workspace. It moves on to looking at the shape of your week and where you can maximise your time and priorities. It ends with broader reflections on how you can make the most of your time at university.

There is always another way …

This section is full of suggestions for different ways of getting organised so you can use your time effectively. Try some of these ideas, and if they don't work for you, find some more to try – ask around. You will be amazed at the things people come up with, and one, just one, might do the trick for you!

The essential toolkit

The essentials of time management are not complicated – the tricky part is working out a system that works for you. Here they are:

- ☑ Writing TO DO lists
- ☑ Using a diary
- ☑ Getting organised

Essential! Lets you sleep at night ...

Writing TO DO lists

Write lists:

- ▶ for the week
- ▶ for each day.

Start with your TO DO list for the week. List everything you have to do by the end of the week. Sweep across the whole of your life: kids, dentist, buying a birthday card ... finding articles, reading chapters, completing coursework ... everything, big and small, from all parts of your life – work, study, personal and family.

Then write your TO DO list for today – again, everything big and small: find that particular article, read Chapter 3, email xyz, pop out and get xx in the lunch hour, dentist (again) …

I have a daily list that includes 'what is on my plate' at the moment. I try to check off one thing in each category.

Put them in a list, and tick them off when you have done each one. It's important to have small tasks: first, because they can be ticked off easily, and second, so you can fit them into short periods between coffee and lecture, lecture and bus … Plus the process of listing everything may well make you feel more in control of it all. Aim to have them all ticked by the end of the day.

I cheat a bit. I tick off a couple of little things I've just done. ☺…

Carry over any remaining TO DOs to tomorrow, include them in your list, and tick them off as you do them. Watch out for any item that you carry over more than three times. What is the reason?

▶ Is it too big to do in a day? Break it down into smaller chunks and list them.
▶ Do you feel stressed about it for some reason? Take the first step today. Find a moment in the day and look at it. Don't try to do it – just look at it.
▶ Tomorrow, look at it again, and write down the first action you need to take to start on it.

If you find you regularly carry over too many, ask yourself *Am I being too ambitious about what I can do in a day?* Try to be more realistic tomorrow.

At the end of what you think of as your 'working week', check what you have done and what is still to do. Then write a TO DO list for next week.

Try it! All you need is a pen (or pencil) and paper …

If you use your phone or laptop for organising things, you may like to explore software designed to help you capture and coordinate your TO DO lists. Simple apps for your phone like 'Remember the Milk' (see 'Useful sources', p. 116) let you list tasks, set due dates, get email or text reminders, and synchronise with your online calendar. Systems such as 'Getting Things Done' can be used with pencil and paper or various software packages.

Getting Things Done

Getting Things Done (GTD) is a time management methodology developed by David Allen. It develops the simple TO DO list into a system: capture, organise, do, review:

▸ **Capture:** a full 'mind sweep' of getting everything you need to do out of your head and 'parked', so that it leaves your brain free to think clearly. If it will take less than 2 minutes, do it straight away.

- **Organise:** other items are organised into 'TO DO' lists by project or by where you will do them, each one with the next specific action to take.
- **Do it!** And tick it off.
- **Review:** each week, prioritise and keep it all moving.

To organise your lists you can use GTD software or a simple notebook or cards and pen or pencil.

Like any time management method, some people find it overcomplicated, and other people love it!

Using a diary

Get a diary, yes – but use it too! Big, little, phone, online … whatever suits you. Use it to put down all your commitments, and write in repeat slots each week (like job hours, lecture times) way in advance to avoid clashes. Then add to it day by day. It may sound obvious, but the fact of being at university adds another strand to anyone's life, bringing with it lots of new commitments: a new study schedule, new activities and new people. Adding all this to your life means you need to do something different to keep track of it.

Beyond that, it's up to you. The only proviso is that you get a diary, use it and write all your commitments down – don't rely on your memory, even if it is a good one!

How do you make sure you can see your day and week and keep an overview of the whole semester? Wall planners are great for an overview but you can't carry them in your bag; phones are portable, but easy to turn off or ignore.

Technology can be really useful. One advantage of online calendars, diaries or filing systems is that they often have the facility to switch between multiple views (daily, weekly, monthly) and can synchronise to a number of devices (phone, laptop and PC). Google Calendars, for example (see 'Useful sources', p. 116), can be shared and synchronised between people (good for groupwork). They can be updated by phone, and set to send you text or email reminders (useful if you tend to forget!).

Your mobile phone can be a very powerful time-saving tool – you can set automatic reminders, text yourself key ideas or notes to remember, and photograph covers of books rather than writing all the bibliographical details then and there. You can use it as a mini-computer on the go.

Other people prefer the low-tech notepad and pencil. Online or electronic tools aren't a magic solution – you have to tailor them to suit you, and watch that they don't become more time-sapping than time-saving.

> 'Better running shoes are not going to make you a faster runner if you've never run before ...'
> Merlin Mann, creator of productivity blog www.43folders.com/ (cited in Pauli 2010)

Getting organised

Most people find it helpful to have their own place for work set up somewhere. It may be just a box in which you keep everything you need, so that all you have to do is lift it off the shelf to get going. Others have their own space – a desk or work surface, or part of a table. Having it set up does make it easier to get started …

Organise your files

This is shorthand for 'work out how to keep your papers in an orderly way' – and it is harder than you think. It matters, because if they are in a jumble you:

 ▶ waste time looking for things, and
 ▶ can't see the whole, or the progression in your programme.

You may start out OK – one folder and a pad of paper – but soon you will find you accumulate lecture notes (why don't lecturers use hole-punched handouts?) and photocopied articles, and before you know it you have a jumble of creased papers falling out of a folder and getting scrunched at the bottom of your bag.

Organising your files is about more than just being tidy. It's about achieving mental order, decluttering your environment and your brain, and reviewing what is important, and what is not, every time you sort.

Work out an organising principle, by course or module, such as putting like with like, or putting things in a chronological order (usually by the date you did it or received it). It all helps to clear the head.

Consider using some (or all) of these:

▶ ring binders and folders – different colours for different subjects
▶ box files (avoids having to hole-punch your papers, but can get jumbled)
▶ a folder to carry around day to day
▶ dividers, tags
▶ a hole punch
▶ thin plastic dividers with holes
▶ Post-it® notes
▶ exercise books.

Label your files, and the notes inside – name of lecturer or writer, date, keywords as a reminder – so you can find them later in the term or next year.

Then you need to do the same with your electronic files. Organise your folders by course, work out a system for filing different drafts of your work, articles and PDFs – and decide what you keep and what you delete.

I use a footer to number pages and date drafts.

Most importantly, organise your back-up system! Everyone says it, few people do it, and most people pay the price at least once. Try:

- saving to a memory stick
- emailing your draft to another email address just so you've got it in your Sent mail
- using a free back-up program like Dropbox (see 'Useful sources', p. 116). Designate a folder on your computer and Dropbox can be set to automatically upload the contents of that folder to a remote server so that you can

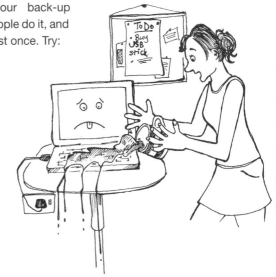

access it from any computer (not just your home one). This means you have an independent off-site back-up.

It doesn't matter exactly how you organise your files – just make sure you do it, and that you have a system that will make sense to you when you look back at it. Check it and tidy it up before the next semester.

'Full time' university programmes are usually drawn up on the assumption that students are 'full time'. This is now often not the case. For many – possibly most – 'full time' students, their weekly schedule reflects a whole range of other roles and commitments – as employee, parent, sports player, carer – of which being a 'student' is only one, an additional one that has to be prioritised because you have chosen to do it.

If you study part time or via distance learning you will inevitably have other commitments, and will find yourself juggling your 'student' identity with the other 'hats' you wear. There may be long stretches of time when you're not being a student or getting onto campus, which can make you feel more removed from university life and studying. Blocking off time to get back to your 'student' identity or forming online study communities are ways of reconnecting.

Your weekly schedule is where all these roles come together. Most likely it will change from week to week as your priorities shift to reflect the changing balance of time you have to spend on each aspect of your life. There will be fixed points in each week (which may be different week to week), other regular commitments that are important to you, and time you can make choices about. The 'working week' (9 am to 6 pm) is just part of the 'full week' of your life.

You've got to keep on top of it ...

Step 1: The 'working week'

Here is the 'working week' of three full time students showing *only* their teaching timetable.

Anita: full time second-year nursing student

	Mon	Tues	Wed	Thurs	Fri
9–10					
10–11					
11–12			Lectures		Lectures
12–1					
1–2					
2–3			Seminars		Seminars
3–4					
4–5		Placement			
5–6					

Taz: full time third-year undergraduate studying social science subjects

	Mon	Tues	Wed	Thurs	Fri
9–10					
10–11					Module B
11–12					
12–1	Module A				
1–2					
2–3				Module A	
3–4					
4–5					
5–6					

David: full time first-year sports and coaching (mature student)

	Mon	Tues	Wed	Thurs	Fri
9–10		Taught sessions		Taught sessions	
10–11		Taught sessions		Taught sessions	
11–12		Taught sessions			
12–1					
1–2					
2–3	Taught sessions				
3–4	Taught sessions	Taught sessions		Taught sessions	
4–5	Taught sessions	Taught sessions		Taught sessions	
5–6					

And here is yours: mark in all your academic/course commitments: lecturers, seminars, lab time, one-off sessions for next week.

Your 'working week'

	Mon	Tues	Wed	Thurs	Fri
9–10					
10–11					
11–12					
12–1					
1–2					
2–3					
3–4					
4–5					
5–6					

Step 2: Your full week

The 9–6 'working week' is a surprisingly small part of the whole picture. Of the 168 hours in the week (7 × 24 hours), the working week (9–6) accounts for 45 hours, and few people work all the hours within it.

When you look at the full week, you see both your additional commitments and the rest of the time in the week you can use.

Here is Anita's full week.

Anita's full week: full time second-year nursing student

	Mon	Tues	Wed	Thurs	Fri	Sat	Sun
5–6							
6–7		Night shift					Travel
7–8							
8–9		Travel					
9–10	Study	Sleep		Study			7.30 Day shift – 8.00 pm
10–11			Lectures and		Lectures and		
11–12							
12–1							
1–2			Break		Break		
2–3		Travel	seminars		seminars		
3–4		Placement					
4–5							
5–6							
6–7	Travel						
7–8							
8–9	7.30 Night shift – 8.00 am	Travel					Travel
9–10							
10–11							
11–12							
12–1							
1–2							

You can see how the fixed teaching times (10–4.30 Wednesdays and Fridays) are a relatively small part of Anita's week (13 hours). Her paid employment is 2 × 12.5 hour shifts, which change regularly, and she has an unpaid placement as part of her course on Tuesday evenings.

By blocking off time for private study on Monday and Thursday, Anita does not waste time deciding when to study. It also means that her study time is confined and doesn't take over the rest of her life, and it brings her total study time up to about 33 hours per week. She can keep Saturday free and has some free evenings in the week. She has some leeway to find additional study time in busy weeks.

Here is your full week. For next week, first mark in your taught sessions, then add:

▶ your other fixed commitments: paid work, travel, picking up kids, other home time
▶ times when you are going to study
▶ other important commitments
▶ travel time – to and from home/uni/placement/work/town
▶ time you choose to spend … however you choose to spend it!

And do build in some flexibility, with overspill/catch-up time in case you need it.

The unexpected is … by definition … what you don't expect to happen.

Your 'full week'

	Mon	Tues	Wed	Thurs	Fri	Sat	Sun
5–6							
6–7							
7–8							
8–9							
9–10							
10–11							
11–12							
12–1							
1–2							
2–3							
3–4							
4–5							
5–6							
6–7							
7–8							
8–9							
9–10							
10–11							
11–12							
12–1							
1–2							

The notion of the 'working week' is a useful point of departure for understanding the kind of time and effort you are expected to put into your studies. In reality, your teaching schedule may extend into your 'full week', using evenings and weekends, and your learning and study time most certainly will. Seeing your week in this way shows how you use your time and how the different aspects of your life can mesh.

Where do you work best?

At home? In your room? In the library? In a café? Does background noise, music or voices help you or distract you? Or is it different places at different times?

Whatever it is, the sooner you work out what works for you, the less time you spend wondering about where to work. If a good place helps you do good work, go for it!

When do you work best?

Are you an early bird or a night owl? When do you work most accurately? When can you think out a general idea for a piece of work? When can you think out the detail? When can you write?

Do not do anything after you have had more than two beers …

Plan to do your most challenging tasks at a time of day when you're most alert, and try to protect this time. If you do low energy things at your best times … all of a sudden your best time has gone!

So …

- do preparatory work at low energy times – admin, collecting sources, finding articles, sorting
- try to move your shifts at work (at least sometimes?).

This is a hard one –

- can you train yourself to work at a different time, if family or work commitments take up your best times?

If you really are a night owl, and you do your best thinking at 2 am in the morning, use this time (but do work out how you mesh with the 'working week' timetable if it includes a 9 am lecture the next morning!).

And which times of day are you seriously unproductive? When your energy is dipping and your eyelids are drooping, try and use this time for:

- preparatory work (see above) or a really short task
- sorting and filing papers
- something active, that makes you get up and move
- a short item off today's TO DO list (like making a call or buying a card)
- emails.

If you really are dozy, take a nap. It will refresh you. But set your alarm for 30 minutes and then go back to work! If one thing leads to another and you don't go back to work after your dip, think about what's stopping you.

Routines are useful. Regular working slots stop you having to reinvent the shape of the week every week (unless you are a shift worker – but if you are, you are probably pretty good at this anyway).

What are your time 'sponges'?

Friends … the internet … checking your overdraft … washing up … iTunes … cups of coffee … sports highlights …? What do you do to put off working? What can you do to avoid these distractions? Try these techniques:

- Turn off your phone and unplug your computer so you're not tempted to check Facebook every 5 minutes.
- Find a place to work that is away from friends or family.
- Use your distractions as rewards – 'I can make that phone call/look at that website once I've …'
- Let your friends and family know when you'll be studying and when you'll be free so they can respect your study time and know when you'll be happy to see them.

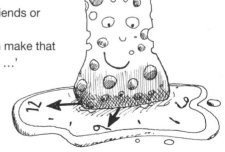

Your personal time sponges	What might work for you

And TAKE A BREAK! Especially an energetic one! A short break of 10 minutes can be enough to refresh you.

A longer break that involves you doing something active can really refresh the brain. After any break you may find that something has just dropped into place, and you're away.

Set an alarm for the end of your break ...

I don't dare stop because if I stop I feel I won't start again ...

I stop in the middle of a sentence. I finish it when I get back and carry on ...

Look after yourself

Look again at your week to make sure you have planned the time to ensure that you eat well, take exercise, get enough sleep – to give yourself every chance of staying fit and healthy.

You probably know this – but at periods of stress and time pressure you can be tempted to drop these important habits just when they are most crucial to you. You do need to plan it in. Try:

Eating and drinking
▸ Look ahead at the day so you can fit in at least one good healthy filling meal, and if you are making it yourself, spot the times when you will buy and cook the food.

Fitness and exercise
▸ If you have a sport or activity you already enjoy, look for opportunities to continue it at university – join a club / use the gym / pool / yoga …
▸ If you don't have existing favourites, try something new … join a class in aerobics / capoeira / rock climbing / salsa / tai chi …
▸ Do it solo anyway – jog / run / walk / swim.
▸ Just get more active in your lifestyle – walk (a little faster than normal?), take the stairs not the elevator, cycle instead of the bus … and so on.

And sleep …?

- This means getting enough sleep for you to function well and feel well – which may be more or less than for people around you. You are the best judge of this.
- Where possible, have regular times for waking up and going to bed – it allows your body to settle into a sleep routine.
- Give yourself time for your mind to relax before trying to sleep – stop studying or looking at a computer screen an hour or so before you plan to go to bed.

4 What do I do first? Prioritising

How do you prioritise? If it was easy, it wouldn't be the problem that many people find it. Yes, you want to go out, but you have that essay to do. What you *should* do is ... well ... obvious, but it usually isn't that simple. Choices are more complex:

▶ Work on the essay ... but it's your friend or partner's birthday?
▶ Do your part of the group presentation for tomorrow (non-assessed), or get on with the research for your report?
▶ Spend time with your child and their homework, or do your own homework?
▶ Use the time you'd earmarked for study, or agree to the extra hours you've been asked to work?

The answers are not easy, and only you can decide. Exactly how intense the pressure of time you are under is likely to be a major factor in your decision.

Questions like these may help you decide what to do first:

▶ What is due in first?
▶ What counts for the most marks?
▶ What is 'added value' and can be left till later?
▶ What can I get done quickly?

- What do I need to take more time to understand?
- What do I need more help with?

Try this:

Now? Soon? Later?

Write down all the tasks that are buzzing around your head. You could just do a random list, or write each one on a strip of Post-it® note.

Draw a big triangle marked like this,  and a bin:

Put each item
in one section
of the triangle.

Now

Ask yourself:
what are the
consequences
if I don't do it?

Soon

Later

BIN IT!
Don't
do it!

Notice that there isn't much space in the NOW box. But then 'now' is … *err* … now – so you have to be decisive. Anything that doesn't go into Now / Soon / Later may not need doing. Can you bin it?

Look at 'Soon' and 'Later' more carefully tomorrow …

This may not work for you, but it might be worth trying once!

The next four pages offer some study advice to counteract some of the time-wasters students report when they sit down to study. To help you focus, here's a task: pick ONE suggestion you might try from each page.

1 Do you waste time looking at irrelevant things?

Read your assignment title or brief carefully and look at the marking criteria — make sure you understand exactly what you have to do before you launch into any research.

Understand your weekly course content. Use your lecture lists to identify the structure of your course and the key topics. Your assignments and exams want you to demonstrate understanding of these key topics.

Keep looking back at your title or brief as you read — ask yourself, 'How is what I'm reading helping me understand my topic?'

Make a list of things you want to find out from your reading to keep you on track.

If it is interesting but not relevant, note down where you found it. You can always come back to it later once you've finished this assignment.

2 Do you take too many notes and find it hard to put them together?

Experiment with spidergrams or cover sheets with bulleted lists to pull out the main ideas.

Set limits to how much you will read and for how long. For example, three books or articles on a topic usually gives a good range of views. Have a deadline for when you'll stop reading.

Put your pen down – only take notes when something is really note-worthy.

Leave plenty of white space so you can add in more thoughts or new ideas later.

Close your book – read and understand first then write a brief overview in your own words rather than copying huge chunks of text.

Group similar ideas together – use highlighter pens, colour coding or sticky tabs.

Use your highlighter sparingly – only for main points and key quotations. A whole page covered in highlighter pen is no use when you look back at it.

3 Do you spend too long reading and researching?

Before you start, know why you are reading. What do you need to find out? For what purpose? Or make sure you have a clear and concise research question.

Allow enough time for finding the sources – it can take longer than you think. Does your library run training sessions on finding information effectively?

But I still haven't found out the meaning of life yet...

Start by looking at something easy to get an overview – an introduction to a textbook or encyclopaedia article.

Read actively. Identify what you want to find out and set yourself questions – look in the texts for answers to these questions.

Start planning your assignment earlier than you normally would do. As you shape your ideas into a coherent story you will see if you need to do more research. This research will be more efficient than your initial reading, as it will be more targeted.

You are not expected to read everything!

Have a deadline for when you'll start your reading and a deadline for when you'll stop reading.

4 Do you find it time-consuming to express your ideas in writing?

Talk over your ideas as if explaining them to someone. List your main points any way you like (bullet points, record them on a Dictaphone) – you can put them into more formal language later.

Plan your assignment briefly before writing – it saves time to know where you are headed.

So, in conclusion..

Hmmm

Write in the number of words you will allow for each section or paragraph. Cutting later takes a huge amount of time.

Write a first draft as the ideas come to you – you can go back and edit them later.

Be prepared for your plan to change as you write – the act of writing helps refine your ideas.

Overcome the blank page syndrome – set a small, contained time, say 10 minutes, to write something ... anything!

Start with the main body. Once you've written a draft you'll know what your argument actually turned out to be, then you can write your introduction to fit.
If you prefer to draft your introduction first to get an overview, make sure you revise it when you have finished.

Sometimes studying efficiently is not about putting in more hours – lots of hard work doesn't necessarily translate into good grades. It is about spending more time on the *right* things. Be active and have a purpose when you study. Study smarter – look at the learning aims and outcomes for your course and see whether what you are doing is helping you achieve these aims.

6 Making the most of university

It is a big decision to come to university – a big time commitment, a big financial commitment. It is also a huge opportunity to do much more than focus exclusively on your studies. Universities offer the opportunity to meet people you would never meet anywhere else (so get to know people from other cultures) and to do things you have never done before (so find out about clubs and networks and join in). The key message here is to get involved in different student groupings, whether a club or campaign – and find the time to develop this aspect of your life as a student.

If you have a regular job or commitments outside university, you will be developing a range of skills over and above those you develop in your academic work: interpersonal skills, organisation, time management (yes!), using your initiative – the 'soft skills' that employers value. There are other opportunities for developing or extending these skills and gaining new experiences during the time you are a student.

With all your additional activities pulling at you, stay aware of your primary reason for going to university. If it is to study, learn and gain a good degree, you need to protect the time to make sure you can achieve this. With so many opportunities it can be hard not to take on too much – it is important to focus on what matters most to you.

So, what are these opportunities? Here are some perspectives on the opportunities university offers:

When hiring graduates I look for relevant experience. If you tell me you want to be a journalist, but have never written for the university newspaper, I'd ask why not.

I have a regular DJ slot on the uni radio.

I'm president of the Kayaking Club – I wanted to do it this year before my workload gets mad in my final year.

I'm a student ambassador. We visit local schools and take school students on campus visits.

I was the student rep on the university working party on greening the campus – energy saving and recycling.

The uni didn't have a capoeira society so I applied for a grant and set one up.

Joining the drama society was the best thing I did – it isn't just for undergraduates!

I ran the Mature Students' Society in my second year. I loved networking with other mature students.

Freshers' Fair was like a zoo and not for me – but many clubs were doing 'taster days' later in term, so I went to one of those.

At university it's all on your doorstep – where else would I have the chance to do circus skills and caving?

Making the most of university 35

Students who leave university with experiences outside their studies will have had a more rounded and fuller experience. If you have managed to achieve this, it will contribute to you having wider horizons and, yes, it will give you some additional points to add to your CV when the time comes for considering your next steps.

If you can see how everything fits together you will be in a better position to make decisions about where and how you want to spend your time.

Part 2 is about getting informed and getting strategic about what you have to do in your course.

GETTING STRATEGIC ABOUT TIME ...

Part 1 was about getting yourself organised, and seeing how study fits into your life and all the other things you want or need to do. The other side of this equation is to see in equally sharp focus what is required of you from the perspective of your lecturers to successfully complete your course of studies.

This section begins this process. It suggests a 'project planning' approach to your studies – after all, achieving a successful outcome to your course is your 'project' for the next year or three. So, if this is your project, let's get going on it and start with getting a clear understanding of what you have to do in the semester or term ahead by:

▶ asking strategic questions
▶ drawing up an action plan.

In any project, you have to work out what has to be done, in what order, by when. This is absolutely what you are doing when you plan your term or semester. You become your own project manager.

The first step is to know exactly what you have to do, module by module, task by task.

7 Asking strategic questions

Six **strategic questions** are often used to work out how to start tackling a task, whether it's planning a project or planning your studies.

Finding the answers to these key questions will help you to see what you have to do in the term or semester ahead. When you can see exactly what you have to do, you can work out the time you have to do it in. This will help you do better, and feel less stressed.

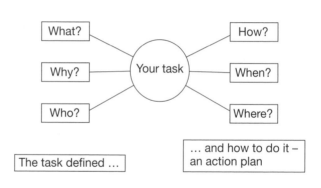

A strategic reading of your course materials

Course handbooks should contain the essential information you need to see what is expected of you, what you have to do and when it needs to be handed in, module by module, course by course.

Some handbooks give fuller details than others. You need to check online as well as hard-copy course materials for all the details and advice your lecturers have set out. Lecturers will, of course, assume you have read them!

What exactly do you have to DO? The task defined

The first three key questions (on the left) will help you find this out.

What exactly do you have to do?	Note ...
Which tasks are **assessed** and which not?	
Is it an **individual** or **group** task?	
Length: word count or number of pages?	
Mark allocation: what percentage (%) does each task count for?	

Why are you being asked to do this?	Note …
External reasons: the 'learning outcomes' you are expected to achieve.	
Internal reasons: your private purpose, your interest in the subject, personal satisfaction.	

Who are you writing for? It helps you write if you can visualise your reader/ audience.	Note …
Your tutor is always your audience. What do you know about what s/he wants to see?	
Do you have another real audience? Like giving a presentation to your seminar group?	
Or an imagined audience? Like writing a report (for a company, for example), or an article for a journal?	

The answers to these questions will help you see exactly **what** you have to do. Now it's time to turn your mind to the practicalities – the detail of how to do it, and the time frame you have to do it in.

How ...? What guidance are you given about ...?	Note ...
What **format** does the task need to be in? Essay? Report? Review? Blog or discussion board post? Presentation? Assignment?	
Any **guidance** about structure, layout and style? Use of appendices? Style of referencing?	

Where ...? will you find the information? ... do you hand it in?	Note ...
How much of it is easy to find (course readers, textbooks, special collections)?	
How much do you have to research yourself, going beyond the reading list?	
And the hand-in: where do you hand in hard copy? Do you have to submit it electronically? Use Turnitin?	

And finally, and most important of all, time and timing:

When ...? is the deadline for the final hand-in?	Note ...
Are there earlier deadlines for drafts and various elements?	

Is anything missing? If you can't find these details in your course documentation, check again. If there really are gaps in the information – ask! You'll be doing everyone a favour.

About deadlines

A deadline is the date and time after which your work will not be accepted without a penalty. It is not a guideline.

If your course handbook says ...

> **Deadline: Week 7 Tuesday 11 March 4.00 pm**
> Electronic copy to Module Leader and hard copy in module box by School Office

... this is what it means.

A deadline is like a train – it passes at a certain time. If you miss it there will be a penalty:

▶ perhaps 10% deduction per day/part of day late
▶ or 0 for that piece of work, even if you are only 2 minutes late.

Plan to have your work completed well before the deadline. Running up to the last moment is just too high risk …

Taking control and looking ahead

Being clear about the answers to the strategic questions is the first step in taking control of the term or semester. Once you can see everything you have to do you can start planning how and when to do it. By defining it, it becomes less scary and you can start seeing your route ahead and how to get there …

Part of this looking ahead involves taking a *really* close look at all the assignments in all your courses, and thinking about what you will have to do and when each phase needs to be done by. This is what Part 3 is about – identifying exactly what you have to do in each module in each term or semester to get the best possible outcome.

PLANNING THE TERM OR SEMESTER

Each term is a journey from where you are now (which might not be the beginning!) to where it ends – when you have submitted all your coursework and done the exams. It is all about time: seeing the time ahead, and seeing the deadlines ahead.

Seeing the semester as a whole, and within it a series of projects that need to be completed, helps you to be more strategic in your time planning. Once you have this overview, it is about seeing the steps you need to take to get each task completed **on time**. This Part looks at the detail of how to do this.

On the next page is a blank timeline showing the weeks of a semester and a column for each course or module to log your deadlines. You may need to adapt it to the length of your term or semester, but you get the idea. A timeline will enable you to see how all your modules fit together and when the deadlines are. Once you can see the whole picture you can work out what you have to do to meet each deadline.

Take a moment to step back and think about how courses are designed. Each course or module has been carefully worked out by the tutors, with essays or assignments designed to allow you to demonstrate your learning – which they can then assess. The trouble is that each module or unit team tends to work in isolation. Even if the main course teams are totally coordinated, students may be taking slightly different combinations of courses that the individual module coordinators won't know about.

The result? Deadlines at roughly the same time in all modules, bunched towards the end of the term – and the prospect of a mad rush to get it all done. This is not a recipe for producing your best work. You need to plan it carefully.

I've got 4 bits of coursework, all due in on 6th December ...

Timeline: planning the term or semester

Wk	Module 1	Module 2	Module 3
1			
2			
3			
4			
5			
6			
7			
8			
9			
10			
11			
12			

and then ... exams?

| 13 | | |

Logging your deadlines

Once you've found out your deadlines you can start logging them on a term or semester timeline.

Take this a step at a time. For now, for each module enter on your timeline:

1 The deadline for each task.
2 How much each task is worth – the percentage (%) of the whole.
3 The word count for each task.

And read on …

Next, we take a closer look at the time planning for a hypothetical student's programme, starting with a completed timeline. We consider some of the major types of task, and comment on the time planning this student will need to do to get it all done – and done well.

We hope that this will offer you some ideas for your own timeline and demonstrate what is involved in getting from where you are now to a good end to the term or semester.

Wk	Module 1	Module 2	Module 3
1			
2	Blog Post 400 words Wed 1.00 (5%)		
3			Critical review 2 articles 1000 words Tues 11.00
4	Blog Post Wed 1.00 (5%)		
5			
6	Blog Post Wed 1.00 (5%)		Annotated bibliography Tues 11.00
7		Group presentation Thurs 2.00 (20%)	
8	Blog Post Wed 1.00 (5%)		
9			Presentation research plan Mon 3.00
10			
11	Individual assignment 2000 words (30%) Submit Wed 1.00	Individual report 1500 words (40%) Thurs 12.00	
12			Research project plan or 'proposal' 3000 words (100%) Mon 12.00

and … then exams?

Wk	Module 1	Module 2	Module 3
13	Exam (50%)	Exam (40%)	

Take a few moments to look at this student's deadlines and consider the implications for their time planning. Some deadlines are distributed through the semester, but the ones with the highest % worth are concentrated at the end. Is this the case with yours?

We now look at the planning this student has to do for a key task in each module. But all the time you have to look across to the other modules to keep up on all fronts ...

10 Planning an individual assignment/essay

Timeline for module 1

Here we focus on the time planning for the individual assignment (worth 30%) in module 1 on page 50. While it is not worth the most in % marks (the exam is worth more), it comes at a busy time of the semester, and could get squeezed by deadlines in other modules – the pressure of the group report in module 2 (20%) and the research project proposal (100%) in module 3.

> *Trawl through handbooks to find answers to the strategic questions (see p. 39)*

> *Blog posts on reading – x 4 every other week. 400 words each. Worth 20% in total. Plan and do every 2 weeks.*

> *Individual assignment deadline Worth 30%. 2000 words. Start planning from Week 6. Will build on reading in posts + more research, thinking and planning.*

> *Exam 50% 2 hours / 3 questions. Revision from Tues Week 12. For more on preparing for exams see p. 65 and 102.*

Module 1														
	Blog		Blog		Blog		Blog			Individual assignment			Exam
Wk	1	2	3	4	5	6	7	8	9	10	11	12		

When do you start working on the essay? In this example, it makes sense to start by Week 6. By now you are well into the course: you will be familiar with the major themes, you've tackled the reading (and posted your comments). It's time to start digesting what you have learnt so far, and extending your research beyond the set readings in preparation for writing your essay/assignment for Week 11.

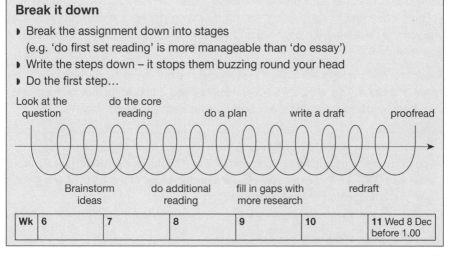

Break it down

▶ Break the assignment down into stages
   (e.g. 'do first set reading' is more manageable than 'do essay')
▶ Write the steps down – it stops them buzzing round your head
▶ Do the first step…

| Look at the question | do the core reading | do a plan | write a draft | proofread |

| Brainstorm ideas | do additional reading | fill in gaps with more research | redraft |

| Wk | 6 | 7 | 8 | 9 | 10 | 11 Wed 8 Dec before 1.00 |

The backwards and forwards of any form of writing is individual and can't really be captured in a list or a diagram. It certainly isn't a linear process when one stage follows another. You may return to some of the stages a number of times – but there is an onwards movement from start to finish.

Time is such an important factor when you have several tasks on the go. You need to set sub-deadlines for each phase. So, for example, stop reading when you have set yourself a deadline to start writing – and write. When you have written your first draft, you will then see what the gaps are and can do more reading to fill in these gaps in your next draft.

Allow time for checking, editing and proofreading before you hand in, correcting all the errors and typos. This will put your lecturer in a good mood when they come to mark your work, and leave them free to concentrate on what you are saying.

> For more on breaking down your assignment and allocating times for each section, you might like to try out the Assignment Survival Kit (University of Kent) (see 'Useful sources', p. 116). You enter your deadline and the type of assignment and it will give you a suggested timeline for completing it.

Meanwhile, you will be only too aware of the other things that need doing: on this module there is the final blog post, and, in the distance, the exam.

The middle of the semester is a good time to get an idea of what the exam involves – look at past papers just to see the format of the exam paper and the type of questions set. This student has the best part of 2 weeks for specific exam preparation between the last coursework deadline and the exam. (See p. 65 and 102 for advice on exams.)

And then of course there are the other modules …

Planning a group assignment

Timeline for module 2

Any module that involves groupwork needs very careful time planning right from the start. Groupwork requires everyone to commit to the work and put effort into making the group work well. You have to pace the work, allocate tasks between you and work to specific deadlines to get work done between group meetings. Of course, when lots of people are involved it never goes this smoothly, so keeping in touch regularly and dealing with any disagreements as they arise is important. Not everyone in your group will be doing the same modules as you; your pressure points will be different, so a last-minute rush is not an option.

> ### Coordination is key
> ▶ Meet early at the start of the assignment.
> ▶ Agree ground rules and meeting times.
> ▶ Assign any roles and divide up the work.
> ▶ Look ahead and plan time carefully.
> ▶ Build in contingency time!
>
> For more on groupwork (see p. 98).
> See also Hartley P & Dawson M (2010) *Success in Groupwork* in this series.

There is plenty of scope for tension in groupwork! But it can be a great way of learning, spreading the load and sharing the research, with everyone working to their strengths.

Your time planning might look something like this:

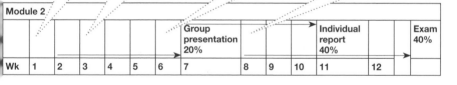

Meet, get to know group members, and establish the ground rules for how you will work (see p. 99) at your first meeting.

Have proper meetings, divide up the tasks and keep a record of who will do what by when. See p. 101. Work out how to deal with imbalances in individual contributions.

Prepare the presentation.

Use feedback from the presentation to focus on further research / gaps to fill. Draft, edit, redraft and check – hand in final report.

Module 2													
						Group presentation 20%				Individual report 40%			Exam 40%
Wk	1	2	3	4	5	6	7	8	9	10	11	12	

The research involved in a groupwork task will follow a similar pattern to the research and writing required for an individual assignment or essay, but with each person doing their section. It will stretch over several weeks and require careful planning.

On top of this, you need to think about how to coordinate your group so the sum total of everyone's contribution is maximised. This involves a *lot* of forward planning and organisation. Other people depend on you managing your own time, committing to meetings and doing your share, just as you depend on them.

Here the presentation comes first. This should focus the minds of the group members – if someone hasn't done their bit, it will be only too obvious to the audience and the tutor. You then have time for more research for your own report.

And all the time you're doing this, you're looking across to the deadlines on the other modules …

Timeline for module 3

This module is really quite different to the other two, more likely to be found in third-year undergraduate or Masters' courses. The dissertation itself will be the focus of the following semester (and most likely through the summer in the case of a Masters' course).

The assessment is also different. While the milestones need to be completed throughout the semester (the critical review, annotated bibliography and presentation of the research plan), the assessment is based solely on the proposal. These other elements are designed to make the student's research footprints clear both to themselves and to the tutor who reads it.

The difficulty in writing a research plan or 'proposal' is not really the writing of the plan itself. The difficulty lies in being able to visualise all the work involved in the dissertation right at the beginning, and setting this out as your 'proposal' before you have really started. Your handbook will probably give you clear advice about what your tutor wants to see in it. It is likely to be some version of: your research question; the reason why you want to research it (or 'rationale'); a brief summary of other research on your topic out there and a short or 'indicative' bibliography; an idea of how you plan to tackle your research; your action plan and timeline to completion.

So in writing your research plan, you are presenting an overall plan for the whole finished dissertation. By the time you hand in your proposal, you will have worked out your time planning for (typically) the following 4 months for an undergraduate dissertation, and 9 months for a Masters' dissertation. It is likely to be the first time you have ever done anything like this (but it probably won't be the last …).

If you're working on a big, long-term project, you need to do something towards it every day.

A longer project needs a different approach to time planning. You don't want to feel you are struggling with some kind of giant octopus, and as soon as you have dealt with one bit, another tentacle wraps itself around you! Nor do you want to over-plan into the far distant future. You want to see the whole, and plan the detail as each phase comes into focus.

Stage 1: Time planning the bigger picture: to dissertation hand-in

Plan this quite loosely, so you can see the milestones and know when you need to reach them.

Your research plan – like any outline – will provide you with a useful point of reference through the journey ahead. Don't try to micro-plan each week into the far distant future – it is likely to be counterproductive and impossible to sustain. Concentrate on the bigger picture. From time to time look back to check that you have moved on, but generally keep your eyes firmly on the major milestones of what you have to do by when.

Try this:

The way ahead

Try to visualise your pathway from where you are now (don't look back and include what you've done up to now) to when you hand in your completed dissertation or project.

→ Take a large sheet of paper – A3 is ideal.
→ Put yourself at the bottom: **start**.
→ Show your completion point at the top: **finish**.
→ Sketch the journey in between.
→ Mark in the phases of the task.
→ Show the trouble spots and milestones – bits you think you will find tricky, bits you will find stimulating, or straightforward.
→ Mark in the time phases (months not weeks).

Give yourself 10 minutes.

Now you have the basis for the overall time plan of your actual research. Write this up as the foundation of your action plan to go into your research plan or proposal.

Stage 2: Time planning the next milestone: the research plan

Now you have fast-forwarded to look ahead at the whole dissertation, you can pull back to refocus on producing a really good research plan or proposal for the deadline at the end of the semester. It takes a lot of willpower to make yourself take the time for this when you are busy with more pressing deadlines …

> *Critical review of 2 articles.*
> The task is designed to help students understand how they should approach the reading for their research.

> *Annotated bibliography.*
> This task is designed to get you to crack into the reading, and show your research footprints to your tutor. Your brief comments will show your grasp of each entry and your thoughts on how you might use it.
> Be selective. Set a limit for when you will stop reading or a target number of essential books and articles to read.

> *Presenting your research plan.*
> Good opportunity to get feedback from fellow students and tutor on your 'work in progress'.
> Build in a bit of time to practise the presentation; this will increase your confidence and make for a more professional performance.

> *Hand in your research plan!*
> The other tasks are all designed to contribute to this, so take it steady. 100%

Module 3													
			Critical review		Annotated bibliography				Presentation			Hand in	
Wk	1	2	3	4	5	6	7	8	9	10	11	12	

This student has some tricky time planning decisions to make – with deadlines for modules 1 and 2 in week 11, when should they aim to get the research plan completed by?

Stage 3: Time planning the week ahead

All the things that need to be done will go onto your TO DO list each week and each day. See pp. 2–6 for more on TO DO lists.

13 Planning ahead for exams

End of modules 1 and 2

When you have worked out the time planning for the coursework deadlines, look at when you will find time to prepare for exams.

Make time to revise

- Look ahead early on in the semester – when are your exams?
- See how your exams fit with your other deadlines.
- Look at past exam papers (if they are available) early on – ideally mid-semester.
- Decide how to divide your time between your coursework and your revision.
- Have a deadline for *starting* your revision.
- Keep up to date with your course content and notes – it makes revision at the end easier.

  See pp. 102–8

You may need to be brutal sometimes about how you allocate your time between coursework and exam preparation. If your last coursework deadlines are very close to the exams, take a strategic look at the relative value of each to you. If the exam % is much higher than the coursework, you may have to be very strict with yourself about how much time you spend on the coursework in order to allow enough time to prepare for exams. Perhaps this is not such a bad thing! The concentration on getting it done may be a case of where working smarter is better than working more.

> *Do one thing towards the exams early on. Find past exam papers to:*
> - *give you an idea of what the exam will be like*
> - *use topics of the questions as a checklist for understanding weekly course content.*

> *With two exams, this student needs to plan their revision timetable. Think about this off and on through the semester – about how and when to revise. Is the time after other deadlines enough? What could you usefully do earlier?*

Mod 2						Group presentation				Individual report			Exam 40%
Mod 1		Blog		Blog		Blog		Blog		Individual assignment			Exam 50%
Wk	1	2	3	4	5	6	7	8	9	10	11	12	

If you look closely at this student's programme, you will see that their last deadline is Monday of week 12. With a revision week, they have almost 2 weeks to revise for exams … You may not be so lucky!

If exams come hard on the heels of coursework deadlines, you may be faced with tough choices requiring strict time allocation as the end of the semester approaches. You will be able to see this coming right from the beginning of the semester if you follow the advice here. If you can see it coming, you can plan for it …

Time planning for a longer semester

In countries with longer semesters, like the United States, the pattern of assessment may be more predictable. That does not make it less stressful – far from it, the concentration of high-value assessments at the end of each course makes the last weeks exceptionally intense for students, where time management is crucial.

The phases and deadlines in an undergraduate semester may look something like this:

> *First 6 weeks: getting to grips with the content. Reading often based on course 'packages'. Large lectures with the instructor, smaller teaching groups with an assistant. Possibly ending with short answers in class tests.*

> *Some kind of synthesis of the topic. More independent sources. At some point students may have to deliver a seminar.*

> *Heads down and writing a 5000 word paper or project. Everyone in all years is doing much the same. What happens to sport ... socialising ... drama clubs ... life?*

> *Hand in! Final-year students write a longer paper 10,000– 12,000 words.*

1	2	3	4	5	6	7	8	9	10	11	12	13	14

The differences between education systems around the world are often emphasised: 'Oh, *this doesn't happen in …*' '*It's different here …*'. Yet the principles of managing your time apply whatever the shape of your term or semester: getting on top of the structure and expectations of your course and planning backwards from your deadlines. In this respect, the similarities between countries and systems are more striking than the differences.

Wherever you are studying, you need to know exactly what is expected of you and by when. When you have a handle on this information, you have every chance of planning for and achieving success.

15 Completing your timeline

You may already have drawn your own timeline based on the 12-week semester time-line on p. 48 and logged your deadlines. If not, now's the time to do it!

1 Log in:
▸ the deadline for each task
▸ how much each task is worth – the percentage (%) of the whole
▸ the word count for each task.

2 Now you can consider the following:
▸ Do some weeks look overloaded? Can you reallocate some work to other, less pressurised, weeks?
▸ Where can you start to plan ahead? Work out when you have to start each assignment in order to avoid a backlog of work at the end of term.

3 And looking at your weekly timetable (p. 17):
▸ Can you see where in the week you will start to get it done?

4 Then work **backwards** from the deadlines to plan the steps (and time) on the way.

About deadlines again

Have you noticed how printers / computers / university servers tend to collapse under the stress and strain of peak deadline time?

Allow what you think is EXTRA time for:

▶ printing
▶ the queue for binding (dissertations)
▶ missing office hours to get the work date-stamped
▶ difficulties with electronic submission (e.g. using Turnitin)
▶ the university system going down at that critical time ....

It happens, and it does not impress lecturers!

Academics are not sympathetic to the modern-day equivalent of 'The dog ate my essay' / 'I lost the file' / 'My computer locked up' / 'The file got corrupted' type of excuses!

And where will you keep your timeline? On the wall? By your mirror? On your laptop? In your folder? Somewhere you can't miss it, so you see it every day …

So, you've got an overview of your semester and plans for what you need to do, but nothing ever goes quite as you planned. It's the difference between knowing what you need to do and then making sure it happens. Everyone has different ways they use their time – some productive and some not so helpful.

Part 4 looks at some of the common time problems and how to overcome them.

TROUBLESHOOTING

You may decide to read this part straight through. It is more likely that you will dip in and out, only reading the bits you feel could be useful to you. If you do find something helpful, jot down one specific idea to try out.

Timetables and TO DO lists don't work for everyone – this is not surprising given that we don't all learn or think in the same way. So suit your planning methods to your own style.

Do you recognise any of the comments opposite (on the left), and could any of the suggestions (on the right) work for you?

Comments on planning habits

I've tried making a timetable but I never stick to it.

I dislike bullet point lists — my mind just doesn't work that way.

Putting all my deadlines on a wall planner overwhelms me — there are too many!

I have a diary, but I forget to look at it.

I spend all my time making a beautiful schedule — rather than doing the work!

Suggestions

I keep a 'Done' list rather than a TO DO list — listing what I've achieved each day is more satisfying.

I have a folder called 'current work' — everything I need is in there.

I make plans visual — colour, pictures, anything to make it interesting.

Instead of a timetable I work out how many hours I want to spend on each module a week and tick them off when I've done them.

A flow diagram helps me see the stages of my project clearly.

I let my friends know my deadlines and then they nag me.

What kind of planner are you? (75)

'How much time should I spend studying?'

'Full time' undergraduate study is regarded by universities as the equivalent of a 'full time' job, about 35 to 37 hours a week on average, including all your lectures, seminars, lab time, fieldwork, placements, private study. Some weeks it will be less, and in other weeks you may need to put in more hours. On a postgraduate course you are likely to spend more hours a week studying to keep up with the intensity of the work.

In reality, people work in different ways, at a different pace, and have different commitments that determine how much time they have available for study. It is useful, however, to appreciate what universities mean by 'full time' when you plan your own study schedule.

'Where did yesterday go?'

You may know exactly where your time goes (see the 'full week' timetables of students Taz, p. 83 and David, p. 80). But if you're not sure where all the time goes, try this:

Day 1: Yesterday Complete a 24-hour pie showing what you (really) did.	**Day 2: Tomorrow** On the basis of 'yesterday', log in what you plan to do and when.
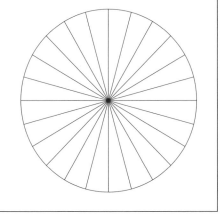	

Stella Cottrell's *The Study Skills Handbook* (2008 pp. 74–7) has helpful activities about using time.

Now look at your 'clocks' side by side. What you are planning to do tomorrow that is different?

Then ... after tomorrow, when you know what you actually did, jot down three bullet points based on your observations of where you could find more time.

How time flies ...!
→ ..
→ ..
→ ..

18 Too little time?

Some university courses, such as taught Masters' and some professional courses, have a lot of teaching time. When this is combined with paid work, family and other commitments, it can seem as though there is no time to fit in any additional study.

Your working week timetable may be full, something like this:

David: full time first-year sports and coaching (mature student)

	Mon	Tues	Wed	Thurs	Fri
9–10		Taught sessions		Taught sessions	
10–11	Work				Work
11–12					
12–1		Collect son from nursery			
1–2			Work		
2–3	Taught sessions				
3–4		Taught sessions		Taught sessions	Study
4–5					
5–6					

David has a full working week. This, however, is only part of the picture. David's 'full week' shows how he uses contained and manageable slots of time for study outside the main working week to good effect, without letting it take over his life.

Fitting in study time before work or uni finds extra hours in the day.

A routine makes getting down to studying easier. It also lets the family know when you are busy — it helps them adapt to your routine too.

Getting into a routine makes studying in early morning or later at night easier.

David has to fit studying in on Saturdays, but has also scheduled football afterwards. It breaks up the day, stops study time from spreading, keeps him fit, and socialising.

	Mon	Tues	Wed	Thurs	Fri	Sat	Sun
5–6							
6–7	Study	Study		Study	Study		
7–8							
8–9							
9–10	Work	Taught sessions	Work – self employed	Taught sessions	Work	Study	Family time
10–11							
11–12		Collect son from nursery					
12–1							
1–2	Taught sessions						
2–3		Taught sessions					
3–4				Taught sessions	Study	Football	
4–5							
5–6							

	Mon	Tues	Wed	Thurs	Fri	Sat	Sun
6–7							
7–8			Work – self employed				Family time
8–9							
9–10							
10–11							
11–12							
12–1							
1–2							

Even though his timetable is busy, David has time free in the evenings.

David has organised his paid work into blocks – allowing him to focus on his paid work in contained bursts.

Blocking off and protecting time for family – they know when you are busy, but also that you will be free later to spend time with them.

Just say 'no'?

It may be that however well you plan your time, become better at studying and more efficient in your life, you simply have too much to do. Something has to go and you have to say 'no' – politely, firmly and with only a brief explanation.

It may help you in saying 'no' to appreciate that this is only a temporary measure, until this particular hurdle – semester, exams, personal pressure – is over. For now, you just need to protect this time to do your best in your studies.

Some university courses do not have a lot of teaching time – especially in the final undergraduate year or research postgraduate courses – leaving you to organise your own time for independent study. It can leave your working week timetable looking very empty:

Too much time makes everything impossible.

Taz: full time third-year undergraduate studying social science subjects

	Mon	Tues	Wed	Thurs	Fri
9–10					Module B
10–11					
11–12					
12–1	Module A				
1–2					
2–3				Module A	
3–4					
4–5					
5–6					

If your timetable looks like this, the challenge is to structure all this 'empty' time in a way that gives a routine to your study. You also need variety – both in your study activities and in other things you want to do outside study to avoid whole days just marked as 'study' stretching before you, something like this:

Using time before and after seminars to study – have to be in uni anyway so maximising the time while you are on campus.

Getting into a routine – regular wake-up time and contained study slots – not too long.

	Mon	Tues	Wed	Thurs	Fri	Sat	Sun
5–6							
6–7							
7–8							
8–9							
9–10		Study (home)	Study (home)				
10–11	Study (library)			Study (library)	Module B		
11–12							
12–1	Module A						
1–2	Group meeting	Study (library)	Study (library)		Study (library)		
2–3				Module A			Study (library)

	Mon	Tues	Wed	Thurs	Fri	Sat	Sun
3–4			Study (library)		Study (library)		Study (library)
4–5	Study			Study (library)			
5–6	(home)						
6–7		Climbing	Football		Prepare for DJ Sat		Run
7–8							
8–9				Catch up (home)			
9–10			Student union night				
10–11					Night out	DJ slot	
11–12							
12–1							
1–2							

Breaking up the week with other activities gives something to look forward to and avoids a whole day of study.

At the start of their PhD, I don't want my students with just noses in books ... I want them in the lab and department too – you can't understand the reading out of context. (Head of Food Science and PhD supervisor)

Some **postgraduates** have little contact time, particularly while they are doing their thesis or dissertation. The thought of a whole day 'reading' can be disheartening.

Mix your research activities to give variety: some study periods for reading, some for preparing to collect or collecting data, some for writing up.

Try breaking down that big chunk of time in the library into distinctly different activities. Finding the material you want to read takes time: using the catalogue, searching using keywords, narrowing down your search to reduce the hits to a manageable list – and then downloading a couple of likely-looking articles … time flies. All this happens before you have 'read' anything! Actually reading an article is a different activity, a welcome one when you have spent a while looking for it. Making notes on it is different again.

Research students often find work in the university: teaching, lab work, consulting. This, while often necessary and definitely useful, is not research! So, while it might start as a way of extending your professional experience and networks, don't let it end up as a time sponge.

20 Missed deadlines and need to catch up?

First of all, don't panic. Most situations are salvageable if you take action, get help, and work steadily towards catching up.

Catch-up checklist

☑ Let your department know
Make your department your allies – if they know you are taking steps to catch up and can see that you are planning ahead, they are more likely to support you. If you keep them in the dark, they won't be as sympathetic.

☑ Is an extension or citing mitigating circumstances appropriate?
If you have a genuine medical or personal reason for missing work you may be eligible for an extension or for your circumstances to be taken into consideration; check your department procedures. But extensions can be tricky if pushing back one deadline backs up all your other deadlines.

☑ List everything you need to do
Getting it all out of your head and on to paper takes away the fear of the unknown

so that you can start to make rational and informed decisions. Identify what you have to do and where you can find the information you need – do you need to ask lecturers or friends for missed notes?

☑ See what needs to be done now and what can wait – be ruthless!

Can making up additional reading and missed lecture notes wait until the vacation when you have more time? (see 'Prioritising', p. 25). If you are working on a project or dissertation, ask your supervisor if you can narrow the scope so it fits into the time left.

☑ Reward yourself for taking positive action

Draw a line under the work you have missed. Keep on going to lectures and classes – you are already moving forwards and taking steps to catch up.

☑ Do one thing from your list

Do something, anything, no matter how small – you will feel better and more in control. Once you've started, it is easier to keep going.

In the absolute worst-case scenario where none of this applies, have the courage to hand in what you have done with an explanation of what happened. Include an outline of what you planned to do, and possible conclusions. You'll get some marks.

Don't just give up and not hand in. Keep going to lectures and do the exams. Hand in what you can and carry on – with a resolve to do better next time around.

Everyone puts off getting started on some things. These then loom in your head as a big cloud that follows you around until you have done them and you can tick them off your TO DO list. And then, magically, they go away …

So what's stopping *you*? Run your eye down the 'Problem' list opposite and see if any of these are an issue for you. Then decide if any of the 'Possible solutions' might be worth a try.

Problem	Possible solution
Don't quite grasp the task / understand the question?	You are right not to start until you are clear about what you have to do – you don't want to waste time. ▶ Look at the wording carefully and see if there is an explanation on another page in the handbook. ▶ Check it against the course outline to see what you should be demonstrating. ▶ Try brainstorming everything you know on one side of paper and then go back to the question. ▶ If it is still not clear ASK someone who is likely to know.
Overwhelmed? Too big to tackle?	Start by breaking it down – list all the sub-tasks and pick one to do first: ▶ find the book/article ✔ ▶ read the summary of one chapter ✔ ▶ read the beginning and end of the chapter. ✔ Set a time limit (10 minutes?) for a short task.
Underwhelmed? Seems too far off or too easy?	Get into the habit of looking at every piece of work when it is set to get an idea of what's involved. Right now, the deadline may seem a long way off. Seeing what each task is asking you to do will help you set a date to start, and ensure you allocate enough time to it.
Don't want to be judged?	Your reader will not see your first efforts, so free yourself up to get your ideas down any way you like. You can do more research, and structure and organise later. When you edit, see yourself as making it an easier read for your reader, not as a piece for assessment.

Problem	Possible solution
Staring at a blank page?	The editor in you is perhaps a bit too busy, and you're deleting or binning stuff before you've got going. Allow yourself to be a writer first (and since it's only you reading it, just write). Then leave it, ideally for at least a day, change hats and become an editor.
Your thoughts wander	It could be that you have got a lot on your plate in other areas of your life. You may be able to deal with issues by listing them and doing them. Or maybe you need to discuss them with someone, or find someone who can listen and help.

But do allow yourself time to think! Learning new things, thinking new thoughts and thinking in different ways is what university is about. Allow time for ideas to settle in your mind and let thoughts go down different paths. Take a break and return to them when you come back to the task tomorrow.

'Sleep on it' is wise traditional advice. Your brain can carry on working it out while you're sleeping! Or when you're exercising. The solution may just pop up …

Procrastination works a little differently from 'can't get started'. It is when putting things off becomes a set of habits that stops you getting down to work: *first I do my email, then I have a cup of coffee, then I phone …, then I sit down and tidy my papers …* And by then you have lost your working slot.

The word 'cras' in the middle of this word is Latin for 'tomorrow'.

I get everything out of the way first … and then there's no time left.

Then come the feelings – frustration, anxiety, feeling angry with yourself, panic, guilt and feeling generally low – which make it harder to get started next time.

Do it differently!

If you can change your habits, can you change your approach to getting started? If you can change just one thing – like not checking email before you start, or changing the place you work in, or the time of day you work – you may find you can break the habit of procrastination.

Here are some changes to their habits that people have tried:

I plan a reward for when I finish a task — a cup of coffee, step outside ...

I tried changing the voice in my head, saying things I'd say to someone like me: Well done / You can do it / That was good ...

I used to think of course tasks as big chunks. Now I divide them up, and list them, and start with the next one thing I need to do.

When I get to this point I list everything I have to do. I pick one small thing that's bugging me and say 'Just do it!' No ifs, no buts.

I like to get outside when I have finished something — get moving.

I put all the papers and print-outs I need in a box lid so it's all there.

I use a timetable now — to show when I will not even think about work.

I put Post-its® on the wall, each one with a small task on it. Then I take each one down when I have done it.

I make it easy to start up again. I stop in the middle of a sentence, so I can get going just by finishing the sentence.

I leave email for when I'm tired.

Changing habits is not easy – you don't know if the change you're making will work for you and you are moving out of your familiar patterns. But then, what you're doing now isn't doing you any good either … so give it a go. Try something different and treat it as an experiment. If it works, great; if it doesn't, try something else!

Like this: *Next time I sit down to study I'll try …*

Trying to polish a piece of work to absolute perfection can be time and energy sapping. The search for unattainable perfection could mean missing deadlines, handing in work late, and losing marks.

Perfect isn't best – finished is best!

But your markers are not looking for perfection … they are looking for evidence of your learning process.

University assignments are about demonstrating your understanding within set limits; the deadline, word count, brief and format (see 'Getting strategic', p. 39) all provide boundaries for you to work within, which mean that 'good enough' really *is* good enough.

Problem	Possible solution
Can't switch off the internal editor?	Trying to order ideas at the same time as drafting each sentence is hard. Separate out these two levels of thinking and try free writing. Set a timer for 5 or 10 minutes and write continuously with no editing allowed. Tidy up the sentences later.
Don't want my marker to think I'm stupid.	Your markers want you to succeed and they are not out to judge you personally. Regard your feedback comments as suggestions to help you … absorb the positive comments, identify what you do well, and pick one thing to work on for next time.
I'll never live up to expectations.	Whose expectations? Yours, your family's, your markers'? You have already proved you are able and competent by winning your place at university. Work to achieve what you want to achieve … not what your friends, family or tutor say you *should* be doing.
Reading just one more book will make the difference.	Markers give most marks for clear communication and good structure. You need enough references to show the evidence for what you are saying, but set limits for when you will stop reading or researching (*I'll finish the reading and notes by Thursday …*).
My writing will never be up to university-level standard.	Keep it simple! University-level work is about explaining your understanding of complex ideas in a clear, straightforward way. Write to express, not to impress.

Thinking time counts as studying time, and it can be as – if not more – valuable than spending time reading. It is worth investing time into really understanding something because this will save time later – you will know how to use the material effectively and will be able to write concisely about it.

The thinking process takes time, so, in a packed schedule, don't underestimate the benefits of making time to think. Block off time to think just as you would block off time to research or write. Use 'dead' time when travelling or waiting to mull over ideas. Or go for a walk or run. Jot things down so they stick in your head – use a notebook, Dictaphone or laptop to capture your thoughts.

When you are thinking it can seem as though you are wasting time, as if you are just generating more uncertainty or going round in circles. But this rich confusion is part of the thinking process, especially if you are working on a research project like a dissertation or thesis.

When you are investigating a topic, your thinking process is not straight or linear, moving logically from one idea to the next. It looks more like a series of diamonds:

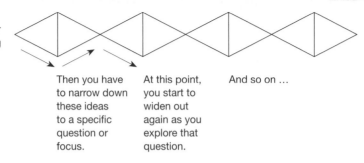

You start by widening out your scope, generating ideas, following up leads, and possibilities.

Then you have to narrow down these ideas to a specific question or focus.

At this point, you start to widen out again as you explore that question.

And so on …

As a Masters' or PhD student you will probably pass through these stages a number of times during a sustained period of research. When you feel your thinking is blocked or not productive it may be a sign to move on to the next stage in the digesting process … do you need to open up your ideas, or focus them down?

(See Williams et al. (2010) *Planning Your PhD* in this series.)

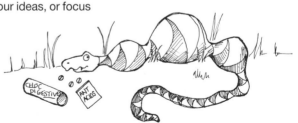

Working in a group can be the best of times, when everyone works together to get the work done. It can also be the worst of times, when people don't do their share, don't even turn up to meetings, and other group members end up doing the work because their mark is dependent on the outcome.

One thing is certain – groupwork is time consuming. Not only do you have to do the task, but you all have to manage a group of people in order to do it. In your time planning, allow for this dual function – definitely more time and slippage time than for an individual assignment.

Here are some suggestions for getting the basics right from day one:

1 Keep in touch
- ▶ Exchange mobile numbers.
- ▶ Share timetables.
- ▶ Know which email each person checks at least daily. The uni one or another?

2 Know the role of your tutor/module leader
What involvement will they (or might they) have in supporting the groups?

3 Agree ground rules

This does not have to be heavy or over-detailed, but you all need to agree how you want to work. Write down the answers to questions like these at the first meeting, and circulate them so that everyone has a copy.

Ground rules

- ▶ Good times to meet?
- ▶ A good place to meet?
- ▶ How will you make sure everyone gets to speak?
- ▶ How will you allocate tasks?
- ▶ How will you deal with disagreements?

What happens if …

- ▶ someone can't/doesn't make a meeting?
- ▶ someone hasn't done their share of the work by the deadline agreed?
- ▶ if you argue?
- ▶ if the ground rules you agree are broken?

---

4 Have proper meetings

Have proper meetings with notes and actions agreed. See page 101 for an Actions sheet you could use or adapt.

5 Find out what everyone's skills and strengths are

And try and use them. Rotate the less appealing tasks (like chasing and checking everyone is on track) so no one person gets stuck with them.

6 Divide the work up and share it out

Be realistic. The jobs that keep the group running smoothly – like booking a room, writing up notes – also need to be recognised as time-eaters.

7 Agree the steps

Agree the steps and sub-deadlines for the task and plot them on your timeline.

8 Prepare for meetings

Before the meeting, circulate a list of points to discuss or report back on at the next meeting (someone's job to collate!)

9 Enjoy!

Yes! You will do the project better, quicker and with much less stress if you can get the basics right and enjoy working with your group. Go for a pizza, meet for coffee.

How late is 'late'?

Actions

Group members: _____

Group's research/topic: _____

Meeting no. _____ Date/time _____ Place _____

Who present: _____

Points discussed and outcomes:

-

-

-

-

Actions

WHAT needs doing?	WHO will do it?	HOW? Detail	By WHEN?

Date, time, place of next meeting _____

26 Time to prepare for exams?

Exams are all about performance within time limits. Many people find them scary; others actually quite *I'd rather have exams as I'm better at exams than coursework.* like them. And you can prepare: approach exams in a strategic way, concentrate on understanding or knowing key points and practise working effectively within time limits.

University exams are perfect for this. You know the examiner – it's your module or course leader! There should be no surprises in the exam, and you can prepare for it.

Look after yourself

However you feel about exams, they are a time of pressure. The suggestions on page 23 are more important now than ever. This is not the time to give up your walk to college, stop your salsa class, or work through the night fuelled only by caffeine. So … eat well, sleep well, drink water and keep up the exercise and at least some of the activities you enjoy.

Take active breaks in your revision to refresh your brain. Stay fit, stay well and feel the benefits.

Extra time?

Extra time in exams is given to 'level the playing field' in order to ensure that students with specific learning difficulties (like dyslexia or dyspraxia), or students with disabilities that can affect their speed of writing or comprehension, are not disadvantaged.

If you think you may qualify for extra time in exams, contact the exams office or disability advisory service well in advance – ideally at the beginning of the semester. Making these arrangements takes time.

Check out exam papers for the last 3 years

Do this early in the term/semester – as soon as you think about it. Looking at past papers is not about question spotting but about looking at the relationship between the questions and the course content.

You can also use an exam paper as a checklist for topics covered in the course. This can save you time overall by helping you understand the course as you go along, as well as being a revision checklist.

Draw up a revision plan

Work out what time you have and how to divide it between modules. Keep it flexible – be realistic.

Become the examiner!

Try to work out your examiner's mark scheme. In short answers it is fairly straightforward. It's an oversimplification to say that if the question carries 5 marks, you need to make 5 different points in your answer, but it is a reasonable place to start. Marks are allocated for something!

In essay-type questions the allocation of marks will be more on the qualities you show – or so they say! In practice, it is structure that counts:

▶ an introduction showing how you will answer the question
▶ a set of paragraphs in the middle, each starting with a clearly stated point, and
▶ a conclusion showing where you have got to.

The examiner will be reading fast. With just a few minutes per essay, ease of reading = cogent argument!

Become the candidate!

Read the instructions (the 'examination rubric') at the top of the exam paper carefully. When you go into the actual exam, it will help if you know what format and type of questions to expect. In the unlikely event of an unexpected change in the format, you will spot it quickly.

Look at the range of formats for a 2-hour exam:

Examination rubric (paper marked out of 100%)	How long do you allow for ...?
Exam 1 This examination includes 2 sections – each worth 50% of the total exam grade. For Section A, you are required to write on one of the two essay questions. For Section B, you are required to write on four of the eight short answer questions (each worth 12.5%).	Overview _____ Section A essay _____ Section B each question _____ Checking _____
Exam 2 Answer ALL FOUR questions in Section A and TWO questions from Section B. Each question in Section A carries 10 marks, and each question in Section B carries 30 marks.	Overview _____ Section A each question _____ Section B each question _____ Checking _____

Examination rubric (paper marked out of 100%)	How long do you allow for …?
Exam 3 Answer 3 questions. All questions carry equal marks.	Overview _____ Question 1 _____ Question 2 _____ Question 3 _____ Checking _____
Exam 4 Section A is COMPULSORY and it carries 50 marks. Answer TWO questions from Section B. All questions in Section B carry equal marks.	Overview _____ Section A _____ Section B each question _____ Checking _____

Work it out!

1 Work out your overall time strategy

Spend a few minutes with a pencil (or even a calculator!) working out a time strategy for each of the papers above. Decide how long you might need to:

→ look over or read the paper first (at least turn all the pages to make sure you're not missing anything)

→ choose questions (if you have choice)

→ check your answers at the end.

Deduct this from 120 minutes (2 hours) allowed for the exam.

2 Work out your marks-per-minute exam strategy

Now work out how long you have for each question. This means working out your marks-per-minute time budget, which turns into your minutes-per-question time plan.

And clock-watch! Don't skimp on one question to lavish time on another. The first 50% of marks in any question are much easier to pick up than the next 20%.

How much can you write (legibly) in 20 minutes?

If it's some time since you last hand-wrote anything more than a shopping list, write a timed practice question to find out how much you do write under pressure. This will help you plan the length of your answers realistically.

Don't feel you have to write lots of practice answers. Outline plans are also a useful way to map out an answer. Look at a question and give yourself 10 minutes or so to plan an outline answer. You'll get used to doing the thinking and ordering your ideas logically under time constraints.

Try to work all this out in advance: it will not only save you time in the exam but will help you be more focused on your revision, and less stressed about the prospect of the exam itself.

Arrive in good time but not so early you have to listen to other people getting anxious.

Allow time to read the instructions carefully – how many questions? Do you have a choice? Do they all get the same marks?

Check the paper is as you expected and see how much time you have for each question.

Read each question carefully. Take time to re-read, and think about each word till you are clear about exactly what each question is asking.

Take time to plan each answer – a few seconds for a short question or a few minutes for a longer one.

Don't spend too much time on one question at the expense of another.

Stick to your plan and you won't run out of time! Do allow time to check your paper for errors you would kick yourself for making.

Afterwards, forget the exam and move on. Take some time out! Do something active and different.

☺

Part 4 looked at specific issues you may have with how you use your time.

Part 5 looks at wider reflections on reviewing your time management and suggesting how to apply your time management abilities to life after university.

So, how was it? Looking back at the last semester or term, how well did your time management go?

And now it is over, it's the past.

But there is a next time …

After a few weeks' break, the next semester comes along – new courses, new schedule, new tutors (perhaps), and an opportunity for you to make a few changes.

Time to change?

Do try to find a moment to think about the lessons you can draw from the last term or semester. Don't just look at the mark and file your returned work; read and think about the feedback from the tutor, and identify one thing to work on.

Think about your time management, too. Only you know what impact your use of time had on the quality of the work you submitted – it's invisible to everyone else. This is why is it worth thinking about how it went, and what you might change next time.

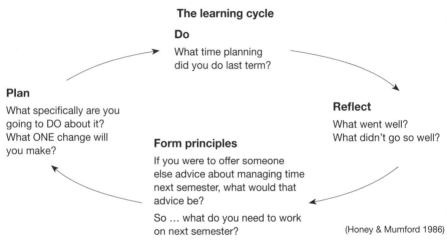

The learning cycle

Do

What time planning did you do last term?

Plan

What specifically are you going to DO about it? What ONE change will you make?

Reflect

What went well? What didn't go so well?

Form principles

If you were to offer someone else advice about managing time next semester, what would that advice be?

So … what do you need to work on next semester?

(Honey & Mumford 1986)

If you find this way of thinking useful, you can try it for all sorts of reflections where you look back on what you did, and want or need to make changes next time around. It is a useful skill to carry with you from your university studies into whatever you do next.

Whatever this holds, it will be different.

You may find that you have too much time on your hands as you lose the structure of the academic cycle and the fixed slots of the working week. We have thought about this in this book and you may find you are better able to build up a 'full week' with things you choose to do because you have already had the experience of needing to organise your studies and deliver within deadlines.

You may find that employment takes out many of the activities you like – so you need to look at your new 'full week' to see how you can make time for activities and people you value.

Good time management is an essential skill for life, and it is highly valued by employers. It is a 'soft skill', along with others you will have had the opportunity to develop in the course of your time at university, both within the course and in your additional activities: the ability to work in a team, to use your own initiative, to see what needs doing and to get things done, to come up with problem-solving ideas. For this reason alone, it is worth working on your time management! It will help you do better, feel less stressed and allow you more time for the things you value.

You know the old saying, 'If you want something done, ask the busiest person'? It could be you …!

Enjoy.